The Long Surprise

Barbara Lau

Texas Review Press
Huntsville, Texas

FIRST EDITION, 2001

Requests for permission to reproduce material from this work should be sent
to:

Permissions
Texas Review Press
English Department
Sam Houston State University
Huntsville, TX 77341-2146

Cover design by Kellye Sanford
Cover art by Susan Coleman

Grateful acknowledgment to the following journals and anthologies, in which
many of these poems have appeared: *Boomer Girls: Poems by Women from
the Baby Boom Generation, College English, Confluence, Field, Icon, Iowa
Woman, Iron Horse Literary Review, Karamu, Looking for Home: Women
Writing About Exile, Poet Lore, Poetry Motel, River Styx, Slant, Southern
Poetry Review, Spoon River Poetry Review*, and *Weather Eye.*

Much sharing of time, talent, and assurances contributed to the making of
this manuscript. I thank and thank: the student, staff, and my faculty
supervisors at the M.F.A. Program at Warren Wilson College (especially
Linda Gregerson, Jean Valentine, Eleanor Wilner, Anne Winters, Renate
Wood); members of my still-unnamed Mt. Vernon writing group (Emory
Gillespie, Marianne Taylor, Amy Shuttleworth, Dan Brawner, Christine
Tabak); rogue poets and best friends Marty Settle and Deborah Bosley;
painter Susan Coleman, for the evocative cover artwork; X. J. Kennedy, for
allowing these poems to slip into his "heart" and onto the printed page; and
especially my husband Don, who introduced me as a "poet" years before I
dared do so myself. —Barbara Lau

Library of Congress Cataloging-in-Publication Data

Lau, Barbara, 1951-
    The long surprise / Barbara Lau.-- 1st ed.
        p. cm.
    ISBN 1-881515-35-4 (alk. paper)
    I. Title

PS3612.A94 L66 2001
811'.6--dc21   2001046247

For Don, Grace & Lily

And in memory of my parents,
Robert Lau and Doris Whitehead Lau

Contents

I
Weight of Being

II
Still Life

III
Terra Firma

IV
Part Vigil, Part Elegy

Part One

Weight of Being

This is just
The stunned interval

After another winter,
The held gasp of surprise
Preceding real wonder.
                              —James Galvin, "Real Wonder"

Joy

is a taste before
it's anything else, and the body

can lounge for hours devouring
the important moments. Listen,

the only way
to tempt happiness into your mind is by taking it

into the body first, like small
wild plums.
                              —Mary Oliver, "The Plum Tree"

Women at the Bath

Degas got it right, sketching nudes
with their backs turned, faces down, absorbed
in the tub's hot tonic. One thousand years of arranged
hips and breasts have not framed such disinterest
as this. They do not gaze at you

with Olympia's mild contempt nor Bacchante's
longing: one leans forward, toweling dry her hair,
one stoops to dampen her sponge, one methodically
scrubs her raised right hip. You cannot tell if they are
pretty, or spent, and the blurred patina of their flesh

gives you no perch to stand on.
Shifting foot to foot, you feel like a nuisance,
a pubescent peeping Tom who might as well slip
down the drain with the dead skin.
Women and water—small surprise,

this broth of insurrection I brew,
the baby fussing in her crib, the husband
half an hour away. I sink slowly,
lids closed, limbs lax. The head grows cumbrous
as a newborn's. The mind loses its compass.

And like a sun-drunk turtle, I begin to float.

Art

My husband thinks there is one right way
    to load the dishwasher. I say
there are fifty good ways to scatter
    the platters, spatulas and mugs.
He gladly demonstrates why *this* space was made
    for plates, *this* for bowls, *this*
for the Cuisinart blade. There's a choreography
    to the flux and flow of water.
But I'm thinking *assault,*

the force of all those suds on my thin white
    demitasse cups; their inability
to duck. Like Janet Leigh
    cornered in the shower on my TV screen—
the blade attentive, well-rehearsed.
    And remember that scene in *Shogun*
where a prisoner's haphazardly
    boiled to death while a Samurai calls his shrieks
song. It's enough

to make me wash and dry each cup by hand.
    But I don't. I'm slip-fingered, and art
is anything but harmless. *Often silence*
    plays the best solo,
my musician husband claims. The headlines
    boast of three separate bombings.
My small life shifts between smashed glass /
    lost keys / spilt milk

and times when my words coalesce
    like cobalt blue spindles
of blown glass. Is chaos
    counterpoint to art, or instead,
its tuning fork? I think the answer

2

matters. I think I'll take a bath
and consider Juliet, who lost
    her timing. And Lear,
such dither and rage.

Rural Nocturne / Iowa

Tonight, the Midwest's dull insistence upon white
makes sense. My headlights spot a picket fence—
it is dazzling, it is hundreds of steeples

scaling the hill. And the blanched farmhouses,
like couplets of lovers on their first night alone,
disclose only what they're willing to show.

Lace drapes each lower window. Upstairs,
shutters (hung breast high) grant glimpses
of bunk beds and heavy-set armoires.

This is the first intact moment of my day.
At home, flowers need weeding, children need
reading to. And the peony's buds refuse to open

while black sergeant ants, mandibles thick
with sap, riot up and down the stems
waiting for one red petal to release.

Inheritance

What to think when we drive past
    three gray clumps of fuzz.
Corpse of raccoon, I conclude,
    because it's September and the young
are leaving their dens. Next month it will be deer—
    bucks in rut, stiff- legged in the ditch
like overturned pitch forks. I'm grateful
    for black-eyed Susans
puddled in the ravines, for goldenrod
    growing in reckless
splendor, for cricket-riddled acres of soy.
    In my tame backyard

wild grapes wait to be jellied.
    Tomatoes darken, swell.
My daughters pick and taste them—
    one tentatively, one wanting
more. If they make me wince
    each time they bolt from the yard
then blame the snake
    for its holy digression,
blame Adam, his lack of improvisation,
    and blame Eve, her appetite
for wine, wisdom, death, flesh: *everything.*

Gluttony

Fat chance you'll release them peacefully,
even years from now. What hunger
made you say, *One is not enough?*
Did the kettle's morning hysteria
really need accompaniment—
one girl shrieking over lost barrettes,
 a second cursing laces that won't submit
to a bow. Excess
everywhere: towers of cold toast, torn leggings
losing hope of ever being mended,
boots blockading your kiss-shove
out the door. Still you crave
the *crescendo and appassionato* of it all.
You need fatigue so keen it chases you
down the foxhole of sleep.
Though it's a scullery kind of love
that stoops to wipe chins and skewer on mittens,
that scoops children into your lap
like a bowl holding sugar. Sweet trap.

Yellow Jackets

If it frightens you to watch them—
    as they lose themselves
        in the split pear—
then *be frightened.*
    After all, it's the querulous end
        of September; the sun
is weakening fast. Come January
    we'll be stunned and strung out
        by the cold. So let them
have their fill. As soon as a pear
    plops off the branch, they are at it,
        ten, twelve of them,
skittering across the freckled green skin,
    searching for the easiest way in.
        Each finds his own warm cave,
buzzing deliriously, toppled upside down
    like ducks standing on their heads
        in water. Even if you hold
the pear by its stem and slowly
    swing it back and forth
        they stay, too absorbed
or too drunk, to let go.
    Like yellow-uniformed soldiers
        on their last furlough home
all they want is pleasure,
    full bellies,
        honey rum at the core.

    (Unlike you—easily distracted,
    accustomed to the taste
of hunger.)

Reprieve

Why he didn't summon her home
but let her roam among the produce, weighing tomatoes;
sniffing the crusted, buttoned-ends of melons;
holding a pair of Japanese eggplants
like little glossy patent-leather shoes,
imagining ratatouille muddling on the stove
as their girls rushed out to play—*later*
she would understand. By now
she's probably staring at columns of ice cream,
wondering whose turn it is
to have her favorite flavor. Then deciding
to buy both, for love hates
to ration itself. Meanwhile

the bicycle has been removed,
and the body of their youngest, draped, and taken.
He sits outside the morgue on a cobblestone bench.
How wise and patient it seems, willing to listen
to any sad tale. He remarks that this fourth decade of life
has taught that all pain comes with a measurable delay,
like the ping-ping of pebbles
against a well's wet wall.
While there's still time he wants to caress

the lovely banality of her thoughts
as she squints to read expiration dates,
total grams of fat. He wants to gild a frame
around this last, intact notion of his wife:
        who splurges on cheap wine,
        who loves all shades of green,
        whose laugh is emphatic and wide,
who now is angling her cart into the checkout lane
and answering, "Paper, please,"
with such calm clarity.

Hieroglyphics (Between Friends)

First snow. The sky's hieroglyphics.
      The air now replete.
    Why must we relearn this year after year:
air isn't hollow
      and flakes aren't mute
    like Kabuki puppets.
Their white rice paper tongues
        nestle on our collars, lips,
    the thin red tips of our ears. *Shhhh.*
Here's the slow drum roll of memory,
      a syncopated shudder.
Here's sound that melts on contact.

(Tell me, when have you been touched
      so slightly? And how slowly
can something fall?)

As children we turned rum-dumb with cold,
      counting flakes great as
barn owl feathers, holding our breath
as they meandered, then landed,
      our crab-apple knees
    knocking all the while. In school
we learned how deer endure winter,
      stripping bark off trees,
    eating blades of snow.
Half of them dying nonetheless.

Better to be geese, you said,
      to leave death far behind.
    Now you're not so sure, since flight—
like snow, like faith—
      takes us to the free-fall zone.
    Let's vow . . . to paint our lips red;

to form a red-rimmed bowl;
        to stay outside until our ears ache,
    our mouths gape,
and we taste the shape
      hollows make
    when filling.

Skirting the Question

Is it a sin to look for logic? --**Martin Settle**

Yes . . . and no.
I might flip-flop down a beach, spot an opal stone with my name
etched underneath, and still not think
    miracle. Or goaded
into a game of pool, unsure how to hold the cue, I might
knock each glossy ball into its pocket, the whole time muttering,
    "Beginner's luck." Then again,
the first yeasty day in May can move us
in unaccountable ways. Take last night, sitting bare-legged
    beside a wading pool, lilacs sugaring the air,
I couldn't have been more content. A new moon
was marooned on the surface. It looked patient and slight,
    nothing like a scythe.
So I dipped in my toe, nudged that slim rim of light and said,
"Profile of God," surprising me as much as you now.
    What to do?
Swat the thought away? Fall down on my knees?
These days there's little room for anything
    in between. Easier to skirt
the question. Watch ice shrink
in my glass. Feel the breeze
    recede. And see
the moon—as moon—
move on.

The Incredible Weight of Being

for Grace

> *The heavier the burden, the closer our lives come to the earth . . . . Conversely, the absolute absence of a burden causes man to be lighter than air . . . his moments as free as they are insignificant. What shall we choose? Weight or lightness?* —**Milan Kundera**

Short on immortality, we build steeples, write books,
have children. Even here at Warren Wilson College,
the Taxidermy Class of 1975 has painstakingly preserved
two dozen native birds in a six-foot glass case.
Bob-white. Screech owl. Flicker. Meadow lark.

My daughter stares in rueful silence.
I try cajoling. The grosbeak, I say, looks short
on sleep. The towhee's still digesting a worm.
But she's reached the inconsolable age of twelve,
weightless no more. And I'm making matters worse

trying to make them better. "That's . . . not . . . right"
she finally says. I know it's not their death
that bothers her most. Our garden snake slipped
beneath the mower's blade. Her goldfish barely lived at all.
Yet they both got honest endings—real dirt, real tears.

Unlike these birds, glued to a perch,
dressed in crocheted capes and vests, bonnets
and caps like Victorian figurines—a prank
played by a secretary down the hall. My daughter's not
amused. She does't know monotony yet,

nor the burden of dictation, nor the cryptic glee
that secretary must have felt, crocheting her little hoax,
fingers swathed in lavender, rose, and gold.

Waking early one day, she ironed her best blouse,
polished her pumps, found the master key

and meticulously matched wing to cape, head to hat,
wondering how long it would take the professors,
the dean, the droll, preoccupied students
to snicker, and forget. "I've been that secretary,"
I start to tell my girl. But I know what she might say:
"And I have been these birds."

Walking Home from the Writing Center

Like the small, kind deceptions
we play on our children each day,

I'm supposed to make you care about
a slim nothing of a comma.

You don't even feel the sinews
of the verbs, the singing of the vowels.

Better to sit with you atop a red silo
mis-naming grasses framing the fields:

moon-raked wheat, copper-lion pelt,
plumes-of-peach-on-charred-tubers;

still finding there are a dozen too few words
to describe October. And of all times to be

struck dumb. I say, trees of sun-dried plum;
you say, pink and gold coupling under gauze.

Ambush

So strange, life is. Why people do not go around in a continual state of surprise is beyond me. —**William Maxwell**

Ambush is how they see it. Not
    crushed seed of pomegranate
    or string of black pearls
    or red clay pebbles spilling down the canyon
    between their legs.

Ambush, they insist—ambush when it comes
    (and I think, ambush when it *doesn't)*
but the six Girl Scouts have stopped listening.

    (Before modesty . . .
    before the need for it . . .
    love was behind every door
    and time was impossible to waste.
    Rain came to make puddles;
    mud was meant to anoint feet, hands, windows
    low enough to reach those small, smudged . . .)

"prints of maidenhood," I begin again,
thinking, anything but *curse.*

My daughter interrupts: "Do birds get periods?"
I reread the paragraph about the mammary glands,
the pituitary, the hidden, patient nest of eggs.
Another asks, "Do we lay them all at once?"

Snickers, then a rush of tongues, hands, wings
    (weaving across the room
        my sparrow, years ago,
    finding the one open window
        with the missing screen).

Post Innocence

Don't be surprised if she says, "I owe you nothing."
She doesn't mean to sound ungrateful,
anymore than the girl who, lacking grace,
blew kisses across the garden wall
and exited, arms loaded down with fruit.
Remember, she wanted for
nothing, never needed to compromise.
Still, she wanted more than he wanted for her—
or less, depending on which version you believe.
Maybe she knew the taste of nectar
would become a burden to swallow.
Maybe she aimed to fashion clothes
from a looser weave.
So take no offense when she leaves
her bed unmade, the stuffed animals
in disarray, to toil
in the soil of her own making.

Girl, Age Ten, Phnom Penh

The chaste way snow straddles
a branch—hovering almost—
how sleep drifts and settles over us.
No clutching. No digging of little heels
in the cracks of the bark. But calmly,
the way he arranges her body
on the bed, the way winter nestled
along the lacy hem of the forest
on his walks home from school. Airbrushed
in snow. And quiet, save for the crunch of boots
across the backbone of the lake. Unlike desire,

that soon grows blunt as a wife's voice
at night, as a daughter's lust for cigarettes
and new shoes. Yet this new body on the bed
knows how to be still, how to drape
her eyes behind black lacquered hair.
If it weren't for her trembling,
he would think she was sleeping.

On a chair across the room, he waits
for some movement to trigger him.
He is in no hurry.
There is no hourglass
for store-front virgins wrapped in
prom dresses. He made her remove
that ridiculous tangle of chiffon
though she clung to it like a toddler to her blanket.

Tomorrow, eight, ten men
might walk through her door. But tonight
would be different. No clutching
at the hair or throat. No braceletting of wrists
to the canopy post. Above the shadows

of his wife, his daughter, he will dance a dance
that chases down desire. Will collect his dowry
of chastity and blood. Holding her now,
slow, steady—hovering, almost.

After Hearing Robert Creeley Read

Open the blinds. The moon is perched outside.
It wants to watch you make shadow puppets
on the wall, and cartwheel
beneath its slender dendrites of light.

The moon can enter you,
but cannot swallow and spit you out, like the waves.
It only wants to make you
playful again. No matter

that your hair is gray and trimmed above the collar—
you are poet of the single raindrop, of *love's watery condition.*
Yet you finger your age like a stain
on your best tie. Did it happen all at once,

the way corn fields overnight turn
from green to whittled bone?
Or more like a stray cat that, once fed,
is determined to stay?

Even with a baby residing in my arms, I
feel the years. It's less about withering flesh
than witnessing too much. At twenty, all good things
are possible; at forty, all bad things are.

Though wild mint still seeps through sidewalks.
Initials still surface in cement.
And I know pleasures so dense
they sedate you. Like tonight, the drowsy

moon, my daughter's face, rocking her to sleep . . .
I could watch her for hours,
I could count every hair
in her moist, black brow.

Part Two

Still Life

Perspective

(five by five by four)

Look, across that field
outlined in thistles
and crushed cars. Is
that
a small cow, head
bowed,
eating grass? Or a

wooden gate, dark with
rain, left ajar? I
choose to see a cow . . .
until you walk through
the field, dislodge two

leaves jamming the latch,
and firmly shut the
gate. Now what's left but
to concede it was
never a cow; it

never lapped dew, breathed
clover, birthed a calf,
or inhabited
a whole acre of
sun, shade, and summer.

Still Life / I

Stop acting like Warhol,
trying to turn that 50-cent can of tomato soup
into a work of art. There are no
sun-drenched-red ponds dotting your table.

~

Oh the weather inside
is frightful. Grown men cry.
Every other Bic pen doesn't work.

(Is it Christmas yet? Can we
string a little mistletoe, fling tinsel at a tree?)

~

The trouble is, I love the children
to distraction. Then the saucepan boils over
and I see red.   (Fine pieta I'd be.)

~

My friend writes to say, "All year our weather
happened inside."
Imagine painting that.

~

My husband is outside, shoveling snow.
It's better than being inside.
The forecast predicts another foot by dawn.

I once called *futility* an ugly word.
He once chopped and stacked wood
for a fireplace we didn't have.

~

In a black section of Charlotte
there's a street named Little Hope.
Seeing it, I never know whether to weep, or cheer.

~

(Is it Christmas yet? Are we home yet?
Can we light just one fool candle?)

Regarding Jean's Decision
Not To Reconstruct Her Breasts

She can ignore the unshoveled snow on the sidewalk;
eventually the problem will solve itself.

Yet those two valleys steam-shoveled
into her chest . . . if breasts could regenerate,

like the velvet lining of the uterus, then fine.
But no more days lost to ether and morphine, no more

dreams of buckskinned, coon-capped
surgeons panning for gold, sieve and picks

poised above her body—not even to placate
her family, her friends, eager for restoration.

Besides, she prefers the word *disfigured* to *prosthesis,*
not a lovely sound no matter how you say it.

Disfigured reminds her of skaters sewing swaths
of figure-eights, and the wine bottle shape

they take for their fast, orgasmic spins,
breasts scarcely larger than hers.

Look, she wants to shout,
death lusts for me, big tits or not:

I wear this patch-work flesh
like war medals on a lapel. I roam

the Art Institute of Chicago, at home among
the cross-hatched cubist figures

until I reach that painting by Bonnard—
not his usual nude, but two plump, honey-skinned

apples placed side-by-side on a plate—
and I ask if that, alone, makes them breasts.

Reduction

for Catherine

Van Gogh shrunk onto coffee mugs. Cassatt pasted onto
postage stamps. Why not us, reduced to long-distance
calls stretched high and thin as Piaf's voice.
Which sense fades first?

The tactile? Or sight bent on fine detail? You try to describe
your newborn's face while I pace the thousand-mile
vacancy between us, inattentive
to my own children.

Would it help to say we've known each other longer than our
mothers knew us? And what, exactly, does that mean? It means
I bought clothes two sizes too big,
not believing I was thin

because I matched my bones against your thinner bones.
That year you wore all white and ran defibrillators up flights
of stairs; insomnia kept you sputtering like a Bunsen burner
half the night.
Most afternoons, we uncoiled

like drowsy snakes on limestone slabs. Now we leave
messages on machines, refiguring the radius of our friendship.
That last night together, our daughters
opened farewell gifts,

did the talking for us. Mine mistook our speechlessness for
anger. She was not all wrong. You say you miss me like a
phantom limb. I match your pace each time I run alone. *Quick,
call me*
with any ordinary complaint.

Positions for Dreaming

Summer Sonnet for Mother

Is this what's left to do—know you
from the outside in? You hid
so well behind the lens, the flash, the quick
click. By process of elimination I deduce
what you loved by what you saved and glued
into this cracked black leather album.
Here, I'm napping in a crib on a sun-
flecked Philippine porch: head drooped
forward, back round as a ball of dough,
bare legs forming a bowl to hold
the breezy head, the sucking thumb.
Did you find grace in the contortions
of a daughter? Did you grin
as you wrote, "Position is everything"?

Still Life / 2

This morning she said, *It's as if you've been sleeping*
all year. Yet tonight you notice everything:
how the youngest are mollified by globs of deviled eggs;
how the oldest drizzle down the hill, clutching their sparklers;
how the adults are pasted onto their blankets,
drunk on *Dos Equis* and the bitter-sweet stench
of gun powder / bug repellent / fried chicken / marijuana.
With each explosion red and blue spiders writhe
in the sky; a woman in a sari
cringes, ducks; the Vietnam vet raises his amputated
drumstick of an arm while you
inch toward that body of dark sparks
you seized ten years ago
like some uncharted continent.

At first you lived on the bread and water
of her love. Each touch took root.
Now she asks, *What can bloom continuously?*
Yet she did! An orchid in a hot house
spilling over the borders of her canvas
like some huge O'Keeffe painting.

You would have stayed in that spot forever.
A drone bee. Hovering continuously.

Then three daughters came in quick succession.
They were so lovely, you could not distract her
from them, your bed now a jungle gym of arms and elbows.
You feel like a stiff, cardboard silhouette
in the midst of constant commotion.
They seem to speak a new language
each time you're away overnight.
You rely on the six holidays in the calendar year
to latch you in place beside them, clasped

in a photo frame, sitting on a blanket,
holding a *Dos Equis.*

What else did you expect? she asked again this morning.
You try, but cannot find words
ignorant and innocent enough.

The Distance a Voice Carries Over the Lake

i / *nude study*

Too cold to be standing here (the bath towel ten steps away) but his
eyes at the window hold me (stark still) drape me in ways (places)
more familiar touches could never reach the high pitch of yearning
his mute body brings this morning (we know better than to rouse)
with one wet kiss across the chain link fence.

ii / *landscape*

How did it start? (A glance?) (A strike of a match?) A *glance like
a strike of a match.* The whole block sweeping October's leaves
into the street and burning them. Then our walk along the fluted
crust of the lake, him naming everything in our path: goldenrod,
marsh asters, Queen Anne's lace, grass of Parnassus, Jerusalem
artichokes with edible roots. I could have stayed the city neighbor
with the commuter husband, calling them all weeds.

iii / *abstract*

The distance a voice carries over the lake.
The time it takes to cross the orchard in the fog.

iv / *profile*

In her cinnamon and cider kitchen, she makes me stay for coffee,
says that's the danger of turning forty—your body finally fits into
itself. Then it longs to peel off the rind of contentment (to shiver
again). She has raised four children and two husbands, but it was
the same for her back then. Watering geraniums, boys away at
school, a friend of her husband's (an occasional bridge partner)
happened by. Dressed in a cream-colored suit, Panama hat, robin's-
egg-blue tie. He took one long swig from the hose, loosened his tie,
smiled a smile that loitered longer than any decent one should. She
knew if she smiled back, took a sip, inched toward her back door . . . .

v / *cubbist landscape*

Ten degrees below. Sizzle of atoms constricting. Forest of chipped
glass and bone. Not knowing if the lake would hold.

Spring Comes to the Institute of Higher Learning

for Deborah

Only the entrails of snow are left.
Boys loll about campus, draping themselves
at the base of statues and dry fountains,
shirts unbuttoned to their sleek Apollo chests.
If they deigned to play softball, it would be slow pitch

though today they grin and swat at each other,
ready to claim their share of the world.
A morsel, really, though who am I,
invisible bystander, to break the news.
If they seek no more than what's expedient—
what feeds the flesh, the pocket—

are they any worse than me wanting spring
to hoodwink this thick layer of years
that clings like chalk, that makes me stare, disbelieving,
at the image in the mirror: a counterfeit
of what's inside—part cobra, part flute,
part dance of sun, shadow, trance.

Aubade/Iowa

October, 9 a.m., two hundred miles from the nearest
skyscraper, the sky
is a stillborn blue. Aphid-white stalks
of corn, dry as parchment, sizzle in the fields,
quieter now that the crickets have fled.

I credit my daughter for this morning's lapse
into slow motion. We meander five miles
on dirt and gravel, headed for Venda's,
the only sitter she will tolerate.
Try driving faster than thirty

and you'll spin out like a toy top
on a brick sidewalk.
(I know this for a fact.)
Sometimes the going's so slow,
I ache, I taste dust in every dusty corner.

But Lily's undaunted, starkly alive, whooping
at a tribe of domesticated turkeys.
Their every step is deliberate, emphatic,
almost graceful in their resolve
not to be, rushed. Unlike the five—no, eight, no, nine—

deer clustered along the berm.
Looking perpetually startled, ears taut
as a cocked trigger, expecting, if not danger,
then something short of mercy.
We creep to a stop, mother and daughter watching

doe and fawn watching mother and daughter.
Each waiting to see who will make the next move.
(Have I always been so impatient, so blind?)
I find that highways were built for one good reason
that speed alone can't measure.

Part Three

Terra Firma

Leaving Texas

for Mady

i

Twice I've abandoned the land of terminal summer
and exhausted sunsets. Traded it in
like a used car I was fond of
but no longer trusted.

Texas gorges itself on its own brute size.
"More pioneers died crossing it
than any in other . . . ." Even Whitman
would have sung himself hoarse there.

ii

The Midwest sun politely ripens and recedes.
The moon laps up the residue heat.
Here, there are no landmarks of pain.
I try beginning again—with less, with more
space to sketch the winnowing day.

iii

Peace has no gravity of its own.
Mady calls to say the new neighbors are too childless,
her backyard too quiet without the bleat
of Grace's rusty swing and her summer medley
of carols. I miss

the porch we painted three shades too yellow,
the house we pruned into images of ourselves.
The breezy hammock. The bent mimosa.
The familiar streets I fed and dressed on walks at dawn.

Quadroon

for Lily

Nothing's more blinding than sun on snow.
But winter's over, and my girl plays mermaid
in the tub, knotting her legs into a dusky fin.
Soap, scrub, rinse, scrub again.
Little earthworm, I tease, amazed the soap
won't work. I even flick on a second light
before I recognize this latest sin of omission—
forgetting how little summer sun it takes
to turn her skin brown. My defense

is the connect; we meet layers beneath
the flesh. Not so two hundred years ago.
Bordellos bred for beauties like her, and men loved
a dollop of coffee in their cream.
Just two, quick generations needed
to prod the pigment, plump the lips,
flare the nose into a perfect bow.

In Texas, confluence was easy to see.
But backdrop matters
and she is leaning against my rabbit-white skin
leaning against bleached picket fences
and twice-mowed lawns
and hybrid corn. Iowa
is a petting zoo
breeding the same animals.

Our new dog raises more debate.
Half beagle? Quarter basset?
The consensus is, it's a *nice mix.*
And I will gladly hold the mottled stones
she hands me day after day, watching her
side-step the cracks, sashay away.

You Decide

Call it what you want—revenge; selfishness; redemption.
But it took an act of will to leave him chained outside
beneath a petulent sky. With each determined
turn of the page, I ignored the howls, the blood,
the cat-shit-matted fur. For the third time that week
he had jumped the fence to menace the cats
that winter under the shed. Twice
I soaped him up, toweled him dry, scoured the tub,
washed the towels. Twice was enough.
But not for my daughter, who wailed,"You're cruel, so cruel."
How else could I shackle her only pet, then push her
toward the fuming yellow bus
waiting to tow her out of my day.

I know what you're thinking, what you want to hear:
that I rescued the dog; that I met my girl for lunch;
that I panhandled for forgiveness like a good Christian.
What stopped me was a tale I recalled by my West Texas aunt—
about a dirt-poor migrant who worked their farm.
Mother of six. Husband mostly gone.
Lonnie never had a birthday cake. Aunt Jo surprised her
with a bakery-made chiffon, so light it levitated
over the plate. And the frosting gleamed
like sucked-on gum drops. And six gold, fluted letters
spelled L-O-N-N-I-E across the top. Small wonder

she gasped, then held the prize high above
twelve gritty, sticky, milk-spilling, scab-picking
hands hammering at her thighs.
Not even waiting for the car to drive away,
Lonnie squeezed out the door, locked the kids inside,
ambled down the road, and ate the cake herself.

My aunt savored each bite

in her rear view mirror, imagining what she'd tell
her preacher, her hair dresser, her city-bred niece.
Mimicking the rhythmic licks of Lonnie's spatula-shaped
tongue, fist-sized swallows and marbled lips.
Noting she didn't even bother to sit down.
But *you decide* what to call that Lonnie.
And next, what to call me.

Toss Up

Rain / sleet / then sloppy, wet kisses
    of snow that splatter the glass,
that stammer and drool onto the ledge.
    Flakes cumbersome as Bolivian sloths
haven't a chance when the sky's this
    inconclusive.

I spent half my Texas childhood pining
    for snow. When it finally came,
one friend wore sandals out to play.
    Another snow-angeled it to death.
By noon my snow was mauled
    to mud. But love—

that's another story. Or the same
    depending on which sky you're watching.
Love, the slow tumble.
    Love, the long surprise.
The nibbled lips; brandied nights;
    kisses that drift and settle on your body.

Then the sure melt: his misplaced words.
    My preoccupied hands.
Which is no surprise. But I never figured love
    would be a toss up
one hour to the next.
Like the quick capitulation
    of snow to water to air.

Apology

This summer I blamed the garden,
bearing one edible thing after another. And nights
spent canning cucumbers, beans, peas so sweet
our daughters gummed them like lollipops.
I dropped into bed, dead branch,
too tired to turn and kiss.
                    (How long has it been?)
But we can't waste

what we sow. Last year it was the youngest,
unable to sleep, her lips plump as dark plums
and those arched brows like two crescent moons
toppled onto each other. So much territory
to adore.   *Since when*

have I returned his gaze, my arms dropping
their load of clothes to fold?
This shift of—should I say, *attention*—
took more than a finger prick on a spindle.
                    (The stew boiled down to nothing:
                    the coals carried off one by one . . .)

Where in the vows were we told of this?
                    Should I
apologize? Ask how little
is enough? Or simply watch how far
ripples flow when a stone
skips across water.

Recovering

First, love what is easy to love.
Rain in late summer. Leaves stain-glassing
the sidewalk. A curve in the road; a just-shucked sky.
Blue petunias pouring down the basement steps.

Next, love what is harder to love. The tubercular
cawing of crows. A field of crushed cars.
Small towns where the funeral home
is the best looking building in sight.

Then love what is unlovable. The third snow
in March. Greed after a funeral.
Arriving late to your father's dying.
Your voice, shouting your daughters' names

as if they were curses. Forgive
the voice. Repeat their names, sonorous as a cello,
remembering what made you choose them.
Explain that depression is a bruise

inside the head. *Yes,* it hurts; *no,* you can't see it;
yes, it makes mommy a little numb, a little mean.
Like Cinderella's stepmother, like Ursula the sea witch.
Next time, call me Ursula. It might make us

laugh. We might collapse on the couch, roaring
a hoary-bellied ho-ho-ho. We might sally into the kitchen,
grab a clump of grapes, shovel them into our mouths
and let the sweet, green globes pulse on our tongues, loving it.

Letting the Rice Burn /
Serving It Anyway

Gypsy! Amateur!
    No locus of control.
        Hoping the pot will tend to itself
            and the children will never
remember. Just say

cheese. Reconstruct
    memories: (chocolate kisses
        under pillows; steamed milk
            upon walking).
Umm, umm, good.

Hickory, dickory, dock. Tail
    on the chopping block. Don't neglect
        to think. *Think.*
            (You're supposed to be somewhere
    Now!)

Fast forward
    to the happy scenes. Use love
        as down payment.
            Trust that butter and saffron
will mask the taste.

Introduction

One night the newborn cried so much
    I put her down
    on the living room floor
and walked away.

On the floor, because she could roll off a couch;
    the floor, because her crib
    was by our bed; the floor,
because I had had it.

In the shower I drowned out
    the sound of her.
    I stayed until hot water
turned cold.

She had no rest. Crying steadily,
    she shoved her two-week-old body
    across eight feet of rug
to show me just what she was made of.

(Is this how flour and milk make cake?
    How one raindrop in your palm
    floods the yard? How a child
spills into herself?)

My Sister's Divorce

No use picking the poppies,
especially the baboon-assed orange ones.
Overnight they'll droop like balloons after a party.
And don't be swayed by the star-shaped purple stamen
that strikes—bulls-eye—the core. Luscious, that clash
of amethyst and orange.

If dunes can drift seventy feet in one year,
what's that say about permanence?
Only a foolish man builds his house upon the sand,
upon the gulf coast dunes we trespassed on.

(Did I tell you the joke about the small-time investor
and his spend-thrift wife?)

When my sister calls, we chat about
lending rates, the lost peach crop, the cost
of treating children to a morning of miniature golf.
Sometimes memory squeezes through—Easter chicks
that outgrew their cuteness, or summers spent tromping sand
on every inch of motel rug / couch / tub / table / bed.
Mother and the dustpan stood sentry.
But sand spreads faster than bad news
(and that's no joke).
We even buttered our bread with it.

Tomorrow, when everyone's happy,
I'll tell you the tale about Carol's
divorce. Today I'm preoccupied with petals,
watching their slow disrobe on my glass table:
how they droop and fall, droop and fall
into muddy orange puddles.

What did you expect?

What I didn't expect is their modesty
after such bold preening, assuming
the hue of sunset when it's most aroused.
Nor my lack of resolve (as if on cue)
wanting what shatters at the touch. See how they
bow, shudder, release each time the screen door slams
and another kid arrives. *Hello.*
Good-bye. No use intervening
(children being who they are—hot wired speed boats).

I'm trying to be patient, to weigh the virtues of staying
or going. But the broom and its sidekick
keep popping out of the closet!
Next I'm toting a pan of petals
past two hundred orange eyewitnesses.
What's worse is my habit of playing
"you're hot, you're cold," you're nowhere
near the spot where I can take aim and hit—

bulls eye—the *punch line.*
You're bound to get a rise
when one life trespasses upon another.
My sister, afterall, is a grown woman.
But to live a life without laughter?

I once tried to love a man for his looks alone.
It lasted two months.
Then I discovered what was missing.
Humor! Laughter! Puns buttering the bread,
jokes sandwiched between sex.
I couldn't wait to leave—his long, serious kisses
felt pornographic.

For years it made me laugh to watch Carol
run to greet me, her hair as disheveled as Einstein's.
Last month we met at the gold-domed Palmer House.
She was giving a talk on investing. Her hair

was short and tame. She wore stockings, perfume,
a mirthless gray suit.

I've decided the poppies can stay, can flood
across the whole damn yard. They're no better nor worse
than my need to make everyone happy.
(Did you hear the joke about two blind sisters
who married the same man?)

Too hot? Too cold?
Who am I to be dishing out advice,
like a snake shedding dead skin.
And what more can anyone offer these days
than time, a little time,
for our eyes to get adjusted to the light?

Surprise Endings

I / Mexico *(for Nancy)*

(Yo soy . . . era . . . seria . . . .)
All those weeks spent conjugating
ourselves *(senoritas . . . hueras . . . Americanas).*

And weren't we dauntless then?
We dead-ended on dirt roads and called it *suerte,* luck.
Slept in corn fields under stars thick as spilt salt.
Hitch-hiked to Puebla, bought *tortas* and snow cones
from street vendors; watched the running of the bulls in Huamantla.

Now you're an attorney, and spend your days
in linen suits. And I am teaching in a town
known only for its soybeans.

(Yo era . . . seria . . . soy . . . .) Sometimes at night
on the highway, I turn my lights to dim
then dare myself to plunge into the wall ten feet ahead.
Remembering *(claro!)* how it felt to be succored
in the lap of danger.

II / Early Retirement *(for Howard)*

He has waited twenty years for this—
    for morning to unlatch slowly;
for his tall, clenched body
    to stretch across the couch;
for the vermilion sun to pierce the window,
    pinning him down
like a wrestler, like a lover,
    bathing him in musk-sated waves,
polishing the wood surface of his flesh,
    dulling the memory of T-squares,
keyboards, the buttoned-down humor
of engineers.

Regarding Man's Failure To Hibernate Through Winter

Our snow was not only shaken from white-wash buckets down the sky, it came shawling out of the ground and swam and drifted out of the arms and hands of the trees . . . . —**Dylan Thomas**

Bruised snow. Hollow sun. Rudderless clouds
that squat on our roofs like pigeons.
We were fools not to follow the rabbit underground,
to watch days end before they begin.
Awakened each night by a predator wind
that growls and paws at the last husks of hydrangea
clinging to the long-abandoned screen porch.
Do you call this weather to live in, alert
and sorry? Do you call this a time to birth babies
saying, *Take this in exchange for the hot tropic sea
you left behind.* Try napping beneath this wind.
Shriek *moo* to the black silhouettes
clumped like raisins on their oatmeal fields.
Wave red-mittened fists at dismembered snowmen.
Oh so, so much white
that refuses to melt, that levitates in doorways,
that ghosts across highways, that glues
to the wet wool-scented wedges of our brains
still managing to preserve a memory of color.
A fiction of summer. While rabbits
sleep and dream through their moment of winter.

Rapport Between Full Moon & Self

God knows why I mention you so often, cliché
that you've become. Even if I write *Cyclops's eye*
or *Penelope's lonely, exposed breast,*
am I merely exhuming Homer from the soggy layers
of my subconscious? Maybe I'm smitten
by the mellifluous sound your name makes
when I say, "moonish grin" and "moonstruck love."
Or do I long to learn your native tongue—
Italian of course—so I can sit on a wrought-iron balcony
crooning, "Bella luna! Visione infinita!"

There must be some good reason you pry me
from the dishes and dripping faucet,
then maneuver me like a marionette
down the still-frozen back steps
to the precise spot where the branches parse.
And there you are, center stage, dangling pendant
of borrowed light. Staring at me
with your one good eye while I stare back,
certain we are connecting, certain we are assimilating
some ancient, arcane truth. Just two dumbstruck souls
who repeat ourselves month after month,
who are always losing perspective, who rise,
nevertheless, above the palaver in our lives.

Shock Value / April

for Yusef Komunyakaa

Whoever thought to plant
purple, tangerine & cream-colored tulips
along wind-bitten Michigan Avenue
is brilliant. Surely an unassimilated
Caribbean sensibility
is at play. These colors
utterly disarm winter,
mock the pessimism of umbrellas,
taunt overcoated auditors
too harried to see
that dog-eared, fish-scaled, blue-lipped
winter has gone with the geese.

Did these tulips feel it first—
the hot, erotic twitch
of sun & mud? Now they flame
these jazz-famished streets
like thousands of mallets
primed to play something
saucy. *Hit me*
with a rhythm so swivel-hipped
that every articulate
young / old / brown / black / pale / paisleyed
pair of hands come together, clapping.

Wishful Thinking

If we should wake one morning
    before the children
        and for once not be, impotent
with fatigue but rather
    alert and curious in a fish-nibbling
        sort of way to hear no

footsteps splashing down the hall
    but each other breathing face to face
        alone with 10/20 minutes
to remember that first lean year
    with so little vacant space
        between us

how your room made a table
    out of a black vinyl trunk
        a desk from that same black trunk
a bed from a sleeping bag
    in which we unzipped
        each other to see how well

our grooves, tongues, pegs, flaps
    latched together, how
        my cockatoo plume
hair reddened your
    bare chest
        I could still love well

were we to unzip
    our mommy/daddy suits
        and be thirty-year-old kids again
but this time
    do it
        quicker.

Long Marriages

have their advantages.
Take those times when words evade us—
when we mean to say *rotunda*, or *shoe horn*,
but stand there jabbing the air, *you-know-you-knowing*.
Captives of lapsed synapses
until the spouse intervenes, retrieves the errant word
like an outfielder catching a fly ball.
(Do I remember to thank him?)
Especially when he nods *yes*, *yes* while I plunge ahead,
word still truant as Huck Finn.
Call this just another chore of marriage, tilled
from the soil of familiarity.
A ripening; a collusion of memory
and forgetfulness. A prescience, even,
one telling the other where he is going.
Lucky for me this marriage tolerates silence well,
knowing what interlopers words can be.

Never Mind

Never mind that the past is a done deal
and the future always conspires
to separate us, one by one. Today
we're together, driving through a dry pocket
of sky, rain ahead and behind us.

My husband is steering, I'm reading,
the younger girl is sleeping, the older one singing.
Her vibrato wobbles like her first ride
on a two-wheeler. The other hasn't grown
into her real voice yet. So far

we have taken two wrong turns
but the day is forgiven. We pass
century-old silos, bleached white houses,
and pigs one month shy
of the slaughter yards. Bus loads

of elderly gamblers race by,
headed for casinos on the Mississippi.
But don't remind me. It's a crap shoot,
this hope that both daughters will
grow up unscathed, their love for me

intact. The stream we just crossed is swelling
its banks. My husband will jig for crappies there
next month. I fish out two quarters for the toll booth.
Never mind that good roads cost money, that mist
wraps us tight as cellophane.

Part Four

Part Vigil, Part Elegy

Vigils

(I—for Don)

I don't care about aviation safety claims—
tonight you're suspended thirty thousand feet in mid air
without a net, your life in the hands of a stranger.
Even I have handled you carelessly at times.

I hunt and peck for reassurance. Your shirts occupy
half our closet, and I know the folklore behind each.
This one you swiped from a brother-in-law
in exchange for a bad debt. This one's a footnote
to your soul band days. This one's too small
but it belonged to your father.

You want assurances too. You packed a photo
from one Christmas spent adrift of family.
Heads buttressed together, we wore Siamese grins,
suddenly smug in our selfishness.
Tell me, which white lies

should I use to lull myself to sleep?
Should I claim some days were made just for us,
the way October skies belong to geese?
Or say the muscle of the undone deed has the strength
to wrestle us down to this earth?

I wear your robe, sleep on your side of the bed.
For the night is long and teeming with stars,
each in its coffin of speed and light.

(II—for father)

Home again, and always the seduction of easy
food, quick comforts. A pantry stocked
in triplicate; air conditioning thick as

whipped cream, and enough hot water to fill the tub.
Yet sometimes enough *is enough*
even in the pink-bricked, flat-chested house
where I grew up. Twenty years later,
out of talk by ten o'clock, I insisted on
jogging around the block. He insisted
on keeping sentry at the curb, dressed in slippers,
armed with flashlight and cane.

Was I 35, he 70?
"This is dumb, you're missing the news,"
I yelled each time I passed. He waited; I ran
and ran and yes, it was a strain
seeing him propped up on legs
thin as teeth in a comb
while I ducked in and out
of his blessing of light.

(III—for Grace)

How angry I was with April's parade
of gray uniform days. I dodged ice patches
jogging at dawn beneath stunted buds, missing
my home town. A *real* spring.
Rows of red buds with pelts of deep pink.
Bluebonnets flooding the fields. And roadsides frothy
with color where I'd plunk down my daughter
for her annual wildflower photo.

Now this sun-loving girl—who hates winter's
swaddling of flesh, hates delays
caused by gloves, boots and zippers—is perched
on our porch, dressed in every mismatched garment
from the catch-all stash. She's waving an umbrella
cheering, "Mommy, you've come back!"

As if I had a choice.
As if I'd choose otherwise
knowing how much I resembled April
those years before she came.
The slippery hope. The hobbled days.
Then the steady gallop
of her four-chambered heart.
And now, here, this sweet and weedy
completion.

(IV—for Grace & Julian)

Another year. What more can I bring to the table
but grief? Yet she begs me
to bake cake. To light five candles.
Only blue will do.

He is the polite brother, who never
rips her books or mocks her words.
Cast in crayon, he appears

in every grade school sibling count,
every family portrait she draws—
sprouting fin-shaped wings
or floating, Chagall-like, overhead.

Did they share the same orbit inside me?
Grow wise to the same metronome drone?

One night I hear her talk in her sleep
and I ask if she's all right. "It's only Julian and me,"
she says, "having a conversation about air."

Where does she get this stamina for remembering
a brother she never saw? I admit,
dear son, my foothold
slips.

(V—for mother)

If I could hide in the folds of your skirt, just listening . . .

If I were the cigarettes you lit and lit and lit,
that fit between your fingers like a sixth digit, a tin sword,
a rabbit's foot, an ellipsis to your life . . .

If I were the crowded steamer that ferried you across the Pacific
to join your military husband, no obstetrician on board
and six months pregnant . . .

If I were the fake tortoise comb you wore for twenty years
(the same comb, the same French twist) . . .

If I were the bottle you hid beneath the couch, visiting it four, five
times a night, kissing the rim, the warm
whisky tongue (who knows how long—you hid it so well) . . .

If I were the hymns you played alone Sunday morning
on your cheap play-by-numbers organ
(*rock of ages, holy, holy, holy, Jesus loves me*)
in a dim corner of the living room . . .

If I were the pillow holding your head when the doctors
finally said it wasn't epilepsy numbing your legs, arms, tongue,
but the sheer white, evening-gloved fingers of death . . .

If I were the gardenia from my wedding bouquet—
the one I would have tossed to you, laughing,
with my perfectly poor aim . . . .

(VI—for Howard)

As neighbors go, Howard's my sentimental favorite.
Purveyor of used books; town crier of new jokes;
street corner expert on pound dogs, souped-up cars,

Kurosawa films, "Jeopardy."

My five year old stared at the thirty metal stitches
criss-crossing his scalp and asked if he forgot
to *stop*, *drop* and *roll*. I concede,
knowing there's a brush fire of cells
spreading from lung to brain to bone.

We fight fire with fire, take him jalapeno chili,
ember-red tomatoes, wedges of scorched corn bread—
food while there's still appetite. I loot the garden
for the most swaggering-yellow mums
that, once dried, will live for years.

"For years!" I mutter, wanting to shower his head
with moist petals. But he'd wave me away,
and in his stripped-down Buddhist manner, claim
"Everything's got a shelf life."
Never mind that the night before, he rid his shelves
of expired vitamins, creams, antihistamines.

(VII—for Lily)

So emphatic a sunset
        we stopped the car to watch
            winter kowtow
                    to spring

                we bought the sky's
                    sales pitch
                        for peaches
                            plums
                                melons.

Elegy

(for Julian)

Most stars fade slowly, turning into traces
of pure hydrogen. Just one in a thousand
is brute enough to seize gravity's crush,
to collapse and dig a black hole.
Stephen Hawking can't even count them all,
these dense pockets of fusion.
He might say each becomes a little son,
a little daughter—foundlings
reclaimed from anonymity

But some bodies fade quickly.
My son, you came quiet and tame as a rabbit
who's lived his whole life underground.
Muscle memory is mainly what's left:
your swift kicks;
hiccups three, four times a day.

They claim it's in the cold spots
where galaxies are born,
where matter clusters, cleaves,
leaves an audible sigh. Rapacious,
that radiation that just won't quit.

(Didn't you know—the universe *is* expanding—
we would have made room.)

Condition

I don't need your prodding to be good.
Or a psalm flung at my side. Or for life to unfold
like a road map on my lap. Just promise,
when I die, to piece back together

the shavings of my stillborn son
sealed in a box inside his father's closet,
gleaning the smell of grown man
and well-worn shoes.

Whether the backyard scrim of twigs
bursts into globes of pears that I will pick,
peel and quarter for the remaining children;
whether the outgrown sandal survives the pavement

to fit the foot of the next daughter; whether
the cracked, black walnuts littering the lawn
resurface in a raku bowl, holding
autumn's odor for months;

whether colors restate themselves
season after season
and I and the husband and the daughters live
another year to see them all . . . .

Distillation

(for Howard)

A scent; a voice; a motion across the room—
everything is growing

thinner to him, becoming an idea. Soon
we'll refer to the *idea* of Howard,

trying to recall his rusty voice
and magpie laugh.

How many of us asked,
have you parted the curtain yet?

All hoping for something new,
yet familiar.

Crocuses, 1995

A housewarming gift: one hundred prize crocus bulbs.
As if we hadn't enough to do, the ground already numb
with frost. But you can't just let them die.

We dug thin rows, chanted the haiku speak
of the seed catalogue: *blue ponds floating*
on white snow; lapis buried in each bloom.

The snow came, stayed. I lost the moon
through the frosted panes, missed the sight of my own flesh,
failed to call my brother on our father's birthday.

March arrived, and what impatient midwives
we were. When the spears unlatched,
barely bluer than the gray snow.

Hue of underfed flesh, of bones jutting out
like shovels. I came and went by the back door,
cursed the botanist who brewed them

into such weak tea. Not unlike you, father,
entrenching yourself in bed, refusing to rise.
I couldn't just let you die (could I?)

And I couldn't barter the peace you sought.
And I still can't say whose penance was worse,
or who dismissed who first.

Addendum

Planning. Thrift. Distancing oneself from risk
is what this banker banked on.
Running out of gas on the highway
was a carelessness he'd never commit.
Nor falling behind on payments.
Nor finding a teenage daughter pregnant
right beneath his nose, no, that kind of blunder
would earn little sympathy from him.
Father, I'm guilty of profiting

from all these lapses. Which is not to insist
that I was right and you were wrong.
Besides, you're no longer here
to defend yourself, and my goal today
is to look; *just look.*
But it's hard to see without judging
this vacant stretch of highway. The sky
is a reticent blue that blurs, like truth, at the edges.
No cloud or motion of birds for embellishment.
Only grass, gravel, stubble of corn
reduced to a beige monochrome.

Unremarkable—
isn't that what you'd conclude?
I'd agree if I weren't intent on seeing only
what's in sight. Having relinquished
the unexpendable, and loved in arrears,
and acquired a child by someone else's folly,
I ask less from what's outside. Beige
is also the color of an outstretched, open palm.

It Was Nothing Like an Abortion

More like an empty cup
turned over.
Or a letter, unopened.

    "His file is three feet high,"
    the caseworker said. Meaning
    taller than him. Meaning
    reconsider.

    I had seen him briefly. He had a Mickey Rooney grin.
    We played patty-cake and touched foreheads
    until our gazes went cross-eyed.
    It was the closest I'd ever come to love at first sight.

I remember murmuring *no thank you*,
then crossing and uncrossing my legs,
expelling a polite sigh
while the world nearly applauded
with understanding.

On the Other Hand, November

(for Joanne)

It's a middling month, after October's bonfire
of plum / lemon / amber-lacquered
    leaves leaving us
only the charcoal-line sketch
of trees, and flower beds neglected
    as this box of torn socks.

But I digress, undress the few colors
left: one charred pumpkin,
    two sallow stalks of sage—
hues so flat as to be vague afterthoughts
of color. Even the sky holds no tincture
    of blue, no seraphim of cloud.

And the gray-bearded fields clump together
like crumpled clothing.
    *(So be it—this is November,
this is Iowa.)* Yet you, patient friend,
stare out the same window to find
    "the limbic root of all seasons"

where nothing organic lacks beauty.
You quote the ancients, like wise Tiresias,
    who's been there / done it
and can see past the fast occasion,
the anemic complaint.
    I stand accused, though like Tiresias

I won't be lobbied. November is
a rote school house lesson in subtraction
    (first mother, then father, then fetus) plus
food spoiling on the counter,

and beds going unchanged.
    For thirty days

it circles like a vulture, digressing,
then descending, opportunist
    of the highways, the ditches.
Granted, it is a keen, resourceful,
even necessary creature.
    But beautiful?

Once Summoned, Tiresias Begs To Differ

You! who languish in your redolent,
red pepper-tiled kitchen, robed in fleece
blue as Renoir's children's eyes—
your biggest conundrum is which cup to choose,
which garnish to slip into your mail-order tea
(rind of lemon? seed of anise?)
while the toaster delivers breakfast
dutiful as my seeing-eye dog.

Look, here's what you've been baying for:
a moon-white petal-shedding of the sky,
a shimmery flock of six-sided flakes.
The *reverse* of subtraction—a *reverse assumption* even,
as grace, post haste, assumes shape
and drifts back down to earth,
obscuring the headlines' daily gospel
of shrapnel and tears.
Soon your whole town will be bathed
in sequined shades of white.

(What I see all day—every day—
eyes opened—eyes shut.)

The Water of Memory

Tonight, ice on the window paints the fern
it clutched and covered last winter.
Beads of frost trace the roots and stem,
sketch the long, filigreed fronds, recalling
how they spread, then bowed and stiffened
in their caskets of ice. How they *became* ice—
like one metal welded to another,
like one body rising to meet another.
The pond remembers every figure eight
skated on its sequined back, the fog, every tree it erased.
And the water in the baby's vaporizer
hums the randy, shiny-dime whistle of crickets
that hatched along its bank each spring.

This is the DNA of memory,
how life announces itself in equal portions
of vapor, liquid, solid.
This is why every sound has a pitch,
why half those pitches mimic my children's
perpetual domain of sounds
(the braying gate, the clapping catalpa leaves,
the last rasping suck of milk).
This is how water breaks life open.
This is what little I know about the soul.

Faith

The crazy faith required
to drive down a country road at night
believing a deer won't leap into my headlights
or a chemical truck headed toward me
won't veer into my path
is more than I can coax into a prayer.

Beneath the ecstatic bits
of stained glass,
the communion wafer approaches
and I waver
seeing the price we pay
for imperfection
feeling His love is pitched
from such a distance.

Still the prayer says *surrender . . . adore*.
The only one I've surrendered to
stumbles into my room at night.
Demanding juice. One more song.
Never doubting
her father and I will roll apart
and let her fill the space
she has always claimed
even before birth.

Where does she begin
and I end?
The cry, the rising; the suck, the milk—
this is more than symbiosis.
It is *take, eat, my body*
which is given for you
it is feeding her is feeding me
it is knowing if faith comes,

it will take me in daylight,
it will be like labor
like hoeing
breaking apart the stiff mounds
of doubt my fingers
have poked and prodded
year after year
flesh confirming flesh.

Search for the Albino Deer

for Emory

We hike through the snow-swathed forest
in search of an albino deer
the hunters spotted, and spared.
Gargoyles of ice cling to limbs
stripped of their bark while pine boughs
steeple-chase morning's last sip
of moon. Bent in silence
we scatter corn and wait
like ice fishermen whose vigil
for a flick beneath the surface
is based less on faith than persistence.
Each time the forest shudders
we hold our breath, almost believing
the deer is there—
has been there all along.

Barbara Lau has spent most of her life in San Antonio and Austin, Texas, where she worked as a magazine writer and publications director. She now teaches English and creative writing at Cornell College in Mt. Vernon, Iowa. She holds an MFA in poetry from Warren Wilson and an MA in English from the University of Illinois. Her poetry has appeared in *Field*, *Spoon River Poetry Review*, *Karamu*, *Southern Poetry Review*, *Poet Lore*, *Iron Horse Literary Review*, and other journals, plus the anthology *When I Grow Old I Shall Wear Purple*. She lives with her husband, composer and jazz guitarist Don Chamberlain, and daughters Grace and Lily. *The Long Surprise* is her first book of poetry.